Curious George®
Makes a Valentine

Adaptation by Bethany V. Freitas
Based on the TV series teleplay written by John Loy

Houghton Mifflin Harcourt
Boston New York

For information about permission to reproduce selections from this book, write to Permissions, Houghton Mifflin Harcourt Publishing Company, 3 Park Avenue, 19th Floor, New York, New York 10016.

ISBN: 978-1-328-69557-4 paper-over-board
ISBN: 978-1-328-69556-7 paperback

Design by Lauren Pettapiece
Cover art adaptation by Artful Doodlers Ltd.

www.hmhco.com
www.curiousgeorge.com
Printed in China
SCP 10 9 8 7 6 5 4 3 2 1
4500673269

AGES	GRADES	GUIDED READING LEVEL	READING RECOVERY LEVEL	LEXILE ® LEVEL
5–7	1	I	15–16	520L

George loves mornings. Mornings that smell like waffles are the best!

"I made you breakfast, George!" said
the man with the yellow hat. "Happy
Valentine's Day!"

"Valentine's Day is the day we show
our friends how much we care about
them." George loved Valentine's Day
so far.

"I'm glad the waffle is good, George,"
said the man. "I have something else
for you, too."

George was surprised when the man gave him a valentine card! What a special day!

George made a valentine for the man,
too. It took a long time, but it turned
out great!

George wanted to make cards for all his friends. But that would take too long! How could he make a lot of cards quickly?

Of course. A stamp! But none of
George's stamps was right for
valentines.

Then George has an idea. He could
make a heart stamp from his foam
blocks.

George was curious. What shapes
make a heart? Two half circles and two
triangles worked perfectly!

But even with his new heart stamp,
making enough cards would take too
long.

George needed a way to stamp a lot of cards, fast. Valentine's Day would be over soon.

Maybe George could stamp quickly on
a pogo stick?

He did stamp a lot of cards, but the pogo stick stamp was messy.

Cleaning up took a long time. Now he really needed a super-fast stamper to finish his cards.

A tricycle stamper was less messy than the pogo stick stamper. But his cards got stuck!

Valentine's Day was almost over and
George still had only three cards.
George was worried.

But, wait! The waffle iron was unplugged
and cool. Could that be the perfect
stamper?

George taped his heart stamps over the waffle iron.

It worked! George was proud of his cards and his stamper!

His friends loved
his handmade
valentines.

And he saved the most important one
for last.